*Man's flight through life is sustained
by the power of his knowledge.*

Austin "Dusty" Miller

THE UNITED STATES

# AIR FORCE ACADEMY

## PHOTOGRAPHY BY JIM RICHARDSON

## HARMONY HOUSE

PUBLISHERS LOUISVILLE

Many thanks to the people of the United States Air Force Academy for their help and hospitality during the year of production on this book. Special thanks to Richard M. Coppock, Executive Director of the Association of Graduates (AOG) for his close participation and guidance in the project. Our appreciation also to Tom Kroboth, Editor of the AOG magazine, *Checkpoints*, and to Don Barrett and Duane Reed of the Academy Library. Additionally, members of the Academy's Directorate of Public Affairs, Major Greg Dziuban, Mr. Will Ketterson, and Staff Sergeant Eddie Boykin spent countless hours in writing, coordinating photo opportunities and providing the escort service needed for the thousands of photos taken to complete this book. All have our sincere gratitude.

Additional photography in this book comes from Craig Aurness on page 54; Brian Payne on pages 92, 93 and 95; and David Denney on page 94.

This book was produced for the Association of Graduates by Harmony House Publishers, P.O. Box 90, Prospect, Kentucky 40059. This is the Second Edition, printed May, 1988 by Pinaire Lithographing Corp., Louisville, Kentucky

Executive Editors: William Butler and William Strode
Director of Photography: William Strode
Library of Congress Catalog Number 86-082731
ISBN 0-916509-09-5

# FOREWORD

The Air Force Academy experience is just that — a tremendous opportunity for people to "experience" so many different aspects of life in a manner that cannot be duplicated anywhere else. No institution in the country can give its students the combination of quality academic education, superb military training, diverse intercollegiate and intramural athletic activities, and spiritual / character development programs offered here. Within a framework of excellence and self-discipline, our cadets can grow intellectually, emotionally and spiritually.

While almost every state competed as the site for the Academy, it now seems incomprehensible that any other location could have been considered to host this institution. Anyone who visits these beautiful grounds must wonder if the selection committee somehow was influenced by divine intervention in deciding upon the foothills of the Rampart Range.

This book is designed to give everyone interested in the Academy a pictorial view of this great place. The photographer who documented the splendor illustrated within this book was not associated with the Academy — so his approach in depicting things like the chapel, athletic fields or noon-meal formation may give a different perspective to the meaning you associate with these standards of cadet life.

The Academy provides a different meaning for each person who has had the good fortune of being associated with this national resource. I hope that whatever meaning you have derived from the Academy will be enhanced by the beauty on these pages.

Lieutenant General Winfield W. Scott, Jr.
Superintendent, United States Air Force Academy

# INTRODUCTION

by Lieutenant General (Retired) Kenneth L. Tallman
Superintendent, United States Air Force Academy, 1977-1981

When asked to volunteer my thoughts about what makes the Air Force Academy a special place, I immediately thought of its "Commitment to Excellence." People familiar with the Academy hear this expression frequently, but there still is no better way to describe what this great institution stands for.

The purpose of the Academy is to fully prepare young men and women for the challenges they will face upon entering active duty as second lieutenants in the Air Force. The goal is to provide a substantive academic education along with practical leadership experiences that will be useful to them after graduation.

During these future officers' terms of service to their country, they will be responsible for the lives and well-being of their people and for millions of dollars of resources. The type of leadership they exert over their subordinates and the kind of management they exercise over aircraft, space systems and research and development programs will have a major impact on this nation's defense posture—both on our fighting readiness and the ability to deter an enemy from any aggression against us. When we consider the survivability of our nation and our culture, the preparation of the future leaders of our armed forces assumes an importance that is as critical as any issue facing the military today. Consequently, an atmosphere that fosters a "commitment to excellence" is essential for the Academy to fulfill its responsibility.

The Academy's total commitment to excellence is reflected in its "Four Pillars" concept which emphasizes excellence in academics, military training, athletics and spiritual development. This drive for excellence was instilled in the Academy faculty and staff by the early leadership of the Academy and continues to this day, producing highly educated, skilled and effective officers.

Although many Air Force leaders in the 1950s had strong West Point ties, those involved with the start-up of the Air Force Academy tried to avoid establishing a carbon copy of the programs of the sister academies. Instead, they believed that Academy programs had to address the unique demands posed by an increasingly important air arm. Their objective was to produce an educated and disciplined officer who could withstand the rigors of combat operations and provide the Air Force with exemplary future leadership.

In addressing the academic program, Air Force leaders knew that future officers would need a solid background in engineering and science in order to handle dramatic innovations in technology. But they also felt the academic program had to do more: graduates would need an intellectual foundation in liberal arts to assist in their progressive development toward major command and staff responsibilities. In addition, the modern air officer had to understand the current Cold War climate; he had to comprehend the economic interaction among nations as well as appreciate the relationship between American society and its military. Moreover, he needed a solid foundation in his nation's history and heritage, a knowledge of other national cultures, and an understanding of the profession of arms.

To achieve these ends, Academy officials first examined the academic programs of Annapolis, West Point, foreign academies and those of prominent civilian universities. Academic planners received valuable advice from the faculties of the Massachusetts Institute of Technology, Columbia and Stanford. The curriculum was evenly balanced among the engineering and basic sciences, the humanities, and the social sciences, and included military training and physical education classes. A new dimension in service academy education was introduced by Brigadier General Robert F. McDermott, the Academy's second dean of faculty, when he devised an enrichment program which permitted cadets mastering basic subject material to take advanced courses in the same or related areas. Later, this enrichment program served as the foundation for a program in which every cadet would major in a chosen academic field. Today, cadets may major in one of 25 areas ranging from the humanities through engineering. The core curriculum (now 30 required courses) provides a foundation for personal and professional growth by exposing every cadet to a solid background which enables acceptance of responsibility and reaction to changes in technological, political and cultural activities that might not be possible for the student who is highly specialized. Whether their intent is to be a pilot or program manager, Academy graduates know the difference between Joseph Heller and Albert Einstein.

For students looking to the future in space, the Academy provides the model for undergraduate space education. The four space-related majors combined with overall space research and training make the Academy the nation's leading institution in this field.

The academic strength of the Academy cannot be praised too highly. It is truly one of the top undergraduate institutions in the country, as reflected by the impressive recognition of its graduates. Twenty-seven graduates have been named Rhodes Scholars in 29 years; 75 graduates have been Guggenheim Fellows; 58 graduates have been National Science Foundation Fellows; and 25 graduates have won Fulbright Scholarships. Further, countless others have graduated with honors from graduate and professional schools.

The decision by Air Force leaders in the 1950s to rely almost exclusively on an all-military faculty, like West Point, rather than on a military-civilian mix, like Annapolis, has been borne out by the overall successes of the graduates over time. The intent to provide a constant active-duty role model for developing qualities of strong character and

leadership has been successfully demonstrated. A note-worthy observation by the accreditation team from the Engineering Council on Professional Development in 1978 further attests to the value of the military composition of the faculty. The chairman of the team, while expressing some concern over the frequent turnover of faculty members, cited that a real strength lay in the fact that all of the faculty had extensive practical experience in the same company (the Air Force) which hires all the graduates. The outstanding per-formance by the faculty has also been enhanced through a solid faculty development program consistently supported by every dean and superintendent.

Excellence is the watchword for the Academy's military training and leadership development programs and is attained through surmounting repeated physical and men-tal challenges. The goal is to help cadets develop their individual character and to instill a dedication to the military calling. Under the leadership of the commandant of cadets, the Academy provides the guidance, environment and the training needed to achieve a sense of discipline, honor, duty and service to the nation.

While tourists may associate military training with seeing cadets in uniform on the terrazzo or parade field, the most significant type of military training the Academy pro-vides is the opportunity to experience leadership in different venues. No cadet will forget the experience of participating in Basic Cadet Training—either as an upperclass cadet or a basic (doolie). Other programs such as Survival, Evasion, Resistance and Escape; Operation Air Force; Operation Third Lieutenant; and the Professional Military Studies pro-gram provide a sound basis for a better understanding of self and of the future in the military.

In the early days before the Academy had any upper-class cadets, military supervision was provided by Air Train-ing Officers (ATO): Air Force lieutenants who lived in the dor-mitories with the new cadets and served as surrogate upper-classmen. The first commandant of cadets, Brigadier General Robert Stillman, insisted on having this ATO force of over 250 made up of junior officers from all commission-ing sources: the service academies, Officers Training School, and Reserve Officers Training Corps. He and his deputy commandant, Colonel Ben Cassiday, traveled around the country interviewing the best young officers for these jobs. The selection process must have been sound, because many of those lieutenants picked by General Stillman and Colonel Cassiday rose to become two, three and four-star generals.

Under the commandant of cadets and functioning as the officer-commander of the cadet squadron or group is the Air Officer Commanding (AOC). This person, like the facul-ty instructor, serves as a role model as well as disciplinarian and counselor to the cadets in his unit. Known as a Tactical Officer at West Point and Company Officer at Annapolis, the AOC terminology was copied from the title used by the Royal Air Force. As an AOC for over three years during the formative period of the Academy, I can attest to the interesting challenges, yet tremendous rewards of working so closely with the cadets.

Speaking of cadets at the Air Force Academy, as with any of the sister academies, one must keep in mind their outstanding academic and leadership qualifications at entry. With the competition for appointment so keen, only those in the top percent of their peers have more than a reasonable chance of admittance. The selection process includes a composite measurement of physical, academic and leadership performance, since proficiency in all of these areas is required to meet the rigors of the Academy experience.

Throughout the year, the staff of the commandant is also involved in supervising several airmanship programs. Since flying is one of the things that attracted many cadets to the Academy, as well as being a focus of their future careers, the airmanship activities take on greater importance than most extracurricular programs at the average college or university. In the early days of the Academy, airmanship consisted of a program of navigator training, with pilot training to follow after graduation. Today, pilot-qualified cadets complete a flying program which includes solo flights in a single-engine Cessna aircraft. All other cadets must complete a navigation course in the T-43, a Boeing 737 adapted for navigator training (although navigator wings are no longer awarded at the Academy). Other airmanship programs, which have expanded greatly over the past 15 years, are soaring and parachuting. Today, every cadet in the Academy has an opportunity to solo in a sailplane; and a large majority of them do, with many becoming soaring instructors. The free-fall parachute jumping program has become equally popular and successful, with the Academy jump team, the Wings of Blue, repeatedly winning the National Collegiate Parachute Championship. As in academics, the goal of excellence is never forgotten.

Underlying a cadet's total experience at the Academy is the cadet honor code, with administration of the code primarily in the hands of the cadet wing but supervised by the commandant of cadets and his staff. The honor code at the Academy is similar to those at West Point and Annapolis, with the same ultimate purpose of producing officers whose integrity is unquestioned, and it provides instant trust under all circumstances. There have been recent changes in the administration of the Honor Code which have strengthened the overall system.

Far too often in discussing service academy programs, people tend to minimize the role of athletics and physical education programs. Excellence within a military organization can never be achieved without top-notch physical fitness; and because of the teamwork and self-discipline associated with winning athletic teams, athletics must play a crucial role in a military organization's quest for excellence.

The Academy's total athletic program encompasses a mandatory physical education program, together with either intramural or varsity athletics. Whether intramural or varsity, Academy athletes are pushed hard to win. We firmly believe that intensive intramural and successful intercollegiate programs are vital to a vibrant cadet wing and a strong Academy, generating a sense of pride and high morale and becoming a unifying force for the student body and alumni. Obviously, winning intercollegiate teams also can enhance recruiting and the public image of the Academy. Overall, Academy athletic teams have won almost two-thirds of all sports competitions during their history—an enviable record of achievement.

Perhaps the biggest single change during the Academy's short history was the introduction of women cadets with the class entering in June 1976. During the first year, young women officers served as surrogate upperclassmen, similar to the Air Training Officer philosophy used in the early years of the Academy. Integration of women cadets into the Academy environment was not accomplished without difficulty. However, by the time the first class of women cadets graduated in 1980, most of the traditional biases had been overcome by the realization that women could not only survive the rigors of the Academy experience, but they could indeed excel. Since that time, women cadets have graduated at the top of their class, won Rhodes Scholarships, led the Cadet Wing and earned all-America sports honors. More importantly, they have become excellent Air Force officers.

No discussion of the Academy should lack a reference to the natural beauty of the area and the man-made facilities that complement God's beautiful architecture. From a structural and a spiritual viewpoint, the nationally-recognized chapel is almost too awesome to describe. The entire cadet area, with dormitories, classrooms, library, dining hall, field house, gymnasium and athletic fields, shines with pride, as does the beautiful new visitors center, named after our esteemed former chairman of the board of visitors, Senator Barry Goldwater. In every season of the year, this national resource is a spectacle to behold. When one associates these striking buildings with the memories and achievements of aviation pioneers like Arnold, Harmon, Mitchell and Vandenberg, an even more mystical aura emerges.

No matter how spectacular the facilities, how capable the instructors or how lofty the goals, the real measure of an institution is the quality of its graduates. Looking at 29 graduating classes, the Academy has produced men and women with integrity, with intelligence and with purpose. Graduates have distinguished themselves in peacetime and in combat—winning one Medal of Honor, 15 Air Force Crosses, and 199 Silver Stars. Two graduates are aerial aces from the Vietnam War; 31 are repatriated prisoners of war from Southeast Asia; 151 graduates gave their lives in combat. More than 50 graduates have been selected for the rank of general officer. Moreover, most of the Academy's over 20,000 graduates have served their country with honor and distinction in almost every Air Force career field. Thousands also have served as volunteer workers contributing their time and their talent in communities throughout the world. Most graduates still remain dedicated to the principles and ideals that first drew them to Colorado. Whether or not they consciously thought about their four years of Academy experience during their subsequent years of dedicated service, these graduates have shown their link to the Academy with their own "commitment to excellence."

I am proud to have served as superintendent of this fine institution and just as proud of the accomplishments of its graduates during its short but magnificent history.

# THE CADET HYMN

Lord, guard and guide the men who fly
Through the great spaces of the sky;
Be with them traversing the air
In darkening storms or sunshine fair.

You who support with tender might
The balanced birds in all their flight,
Lord of the tempered winds, be near,
That, having you, they know no fear.

Control their minds with instinct fit
Whene'er, adventuring, they quit
The firm security of land;
Grant steadfast eye and skillful hand.

Aloft in solitudes of space,
Uphold them with your saving grace.
O God, protect the men who fly
Through lonely ways beneath the sky.

*It is a tough school that has grown out of those*
*early years, as the lights burning late at night testify.*

Gen. T.R. Milton, USAF, Ret.

*The beauty of the setting, here at the foothills of the Rockies, evokes the spirit of freedom that is America. And because of that beauty, it is all too easy to forget that freedom is maintained by those who have defended it in the darkest corners of the earth, against the most difficult odds.*

Lt. Gen. James R. Allen, at dedication of Sijan Hall, May, 1976

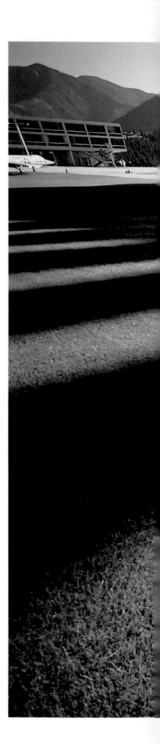

*Basic Cadet training*

*Service academies perform two unique services which no civilian institution of like rank could hope or be expected to do...(first) intense and continued emphasis upon the ideal of service to the country... (second) inspiring their members to high standards of integrity and ethical conduct.*

Dr. John Hannah, at Congressional hearings regarding the establishment of the Air Force Academy, 1954

*With respect to honor, devotion and high standards of scholarship, you have already earned a place in the company of the other great academies which are dedicated to serving our nation and its ideals.*

James E. Briggs,
Major General, U.S.A.F.
Superintendent, The U.S. Air Force Academy

*The Academy Library*

*We are more than the buildings here — more than marble, glass, aluminum and concrete. We, all of us, are flesh, blood, ideas and commitment.*

Lt. General Winfield W. Scott, Jr.
*Checkpoints*, 1983

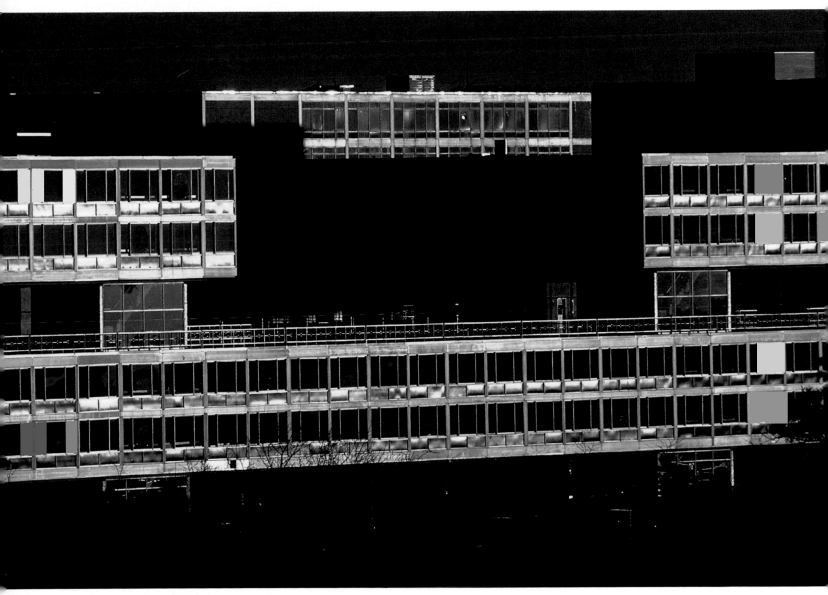

*Sijan Hall*

*We accept the primary responsibility for teaching cadets to express themselves effectively and correctly; we expect them to read good literature with understanding, appreciation and enjoyment. We encourage their interpretive and imaginative powers towards the end of expanding and maturing their minds.*

Brig. General Peter R. Moody, original English Department Mission Statement

*Planetarium*

*Lt. Gen. Hubert R. Harmon statue, gift of the class of 1959.*

*Observatory*

*Jet Engine Laboratory*

*Class in satellite navigation*

51

*Mitchell Hall*

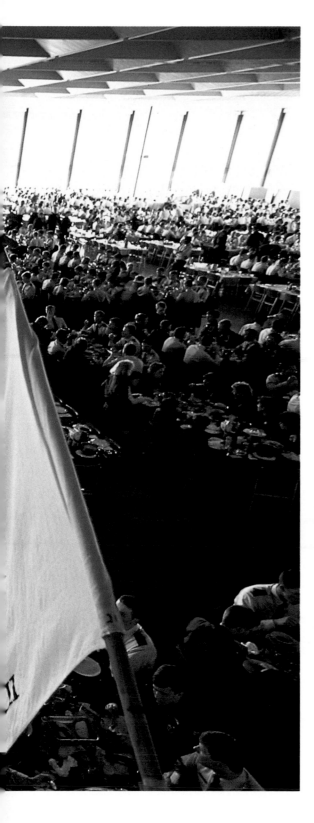

*Room Inspection*

*Drill Team*

*Cadet Wing on parade*

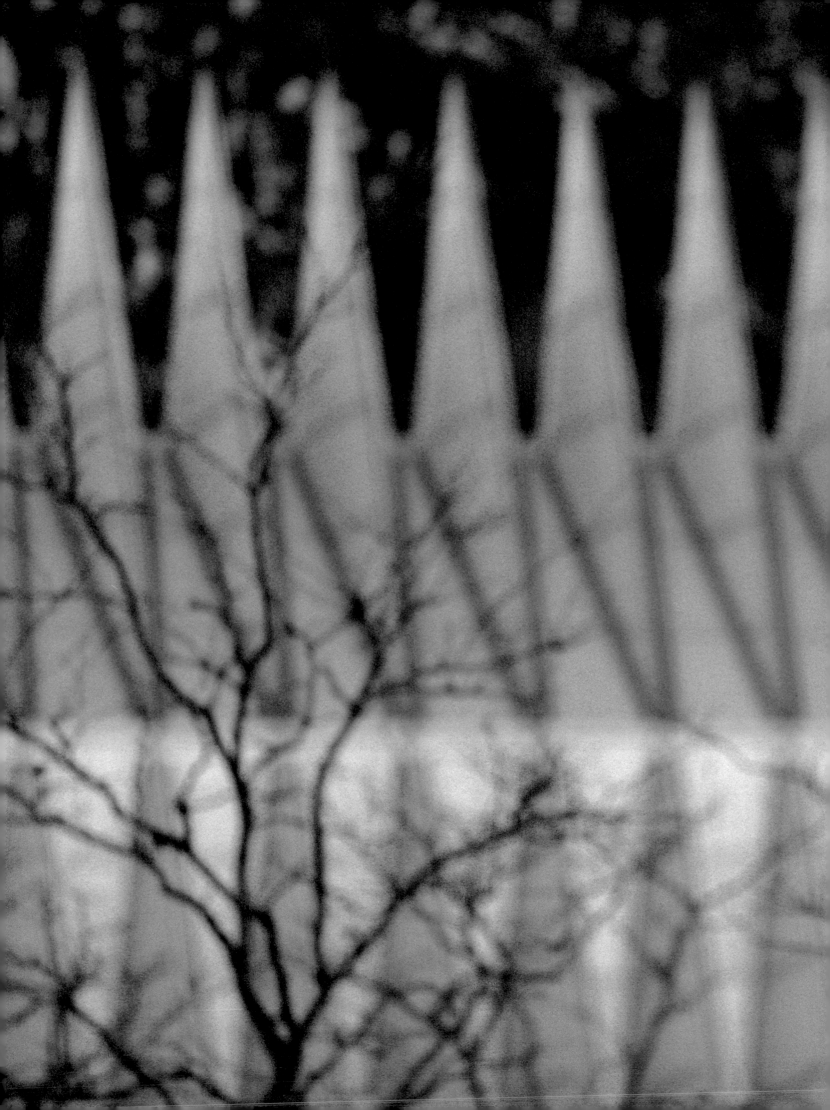

*Cadet Chapel*

*The chapel has grown into one of the most famous
ecclesiastical buildings in the world. Its picture hangs
in offices wherever Air Force people find themselves.
Its structure dominates the Academy and is visible
for miles around and from miles up. Living in and
working in its shadow, one cannot help but be
impressed by its sweep and style.*

Chaplain Theodore Stainman, December, 1973

*One More Roll*

*We toast our hearty comrades, who have*
*fallen from the skies, and were gently caught*
*By God's Own Hands to be with Him on high.*

*To dwell among the soaring clouds*
*They've known so well before, from victory*
*Roll to tail chase at heaven's very door.*

*As we fly among them there, we're sure to*
*Hear their plea, take care my friend,*
*Watch your six, and do one more roll for me.*

Written in 1968 by Commander Jerry Coffee
while a prisoner of war in Hanoi.

*Roll of Honor*

*Your future lives will be shaped inexorably by how you discharge your duties to the Academy, to your service, and your country during your day-to-day life here. You have an opportunity given to few men.*

Gen. Joseph T. McNarney, Address to Cadet Wing, 1955

*Soaring Training*

*Preparation for flight is not enough; preparation for leadership in the aerospace age is not enough; only preparation for a life of service is sufficient for the complex world we will face tomorrow.*

James E. Briggs, Superintendent,
U.S. Air Force Academy, 1956 - 1959

*Flight Simulator*

*Stress Lab*

*My first view of the Air Force Academy site was from a helicopter. We took off from Lowry Air Force base in Denver, and the weather was so thick we had just enough elbow room to snake along the base of the Rampart Range. Then the Cathedral Rock mass loomed ahead and the pilot eased up and over. There was Shangri-La!*

Milton Caniff, 1972

Most visitors have the impression that the Air Force Academy is a flying school. It is no more a flying school than West Point is a skeet range... It's a university.

Ed Mack Miller in *Wild Blue U.*

*October 4, 1958, that's the date the Air Force Academy came of age. It's the day the Falcons met the challenge of athletic greatness and passed with flying colors. The yardstick was applied by the touted Iowa Hawkeyes, proud standard bearers of the greatest football conference of them all, the Big Ten. The score was 13-13 and the result transcends sports in its effect on the Academy. All sports tradition at the Academy now starts with this game. No matter what happens to the rest of the season or in seasons to come, they'll still go back to this game in Iowa City when the Air Force Academy made its mark in the face of great odds.*

Bob Collins, *Rocky Mountain News*, Oct. 5, 1958

*The Wright Brothers decorated for an Air Force Academy vs. Navy football game.*

*On the fields of friendly strife are sown the seeds that on other days...*

*...and other fields will bear the fruits of victory.* General Douglas MacArthur

*I see the faces of my classmates who are no longer here; the faces of those who have given their lives in the defense of this nation. To me, that is the sum and substance as to why we are gathered here today — to dedicate a place of remembrance; a remembrance that the citizens of this nation had the foresight to establish, an institution whose fundamental purpose was to train and inspire young men and women to the higher principles of duty, honor and country over the preservation of their own lives. I am fully confident that the spirits of these fellow cadets will rise, and cause countless other graduates of this Air Force Academy, if called, to proudly hold aloft the red, white and blue in this country's defense.*

Col. Bob Beckel, '59 at dedication of the Air Force
Academy marker at Lowry Air Force Base, 1979

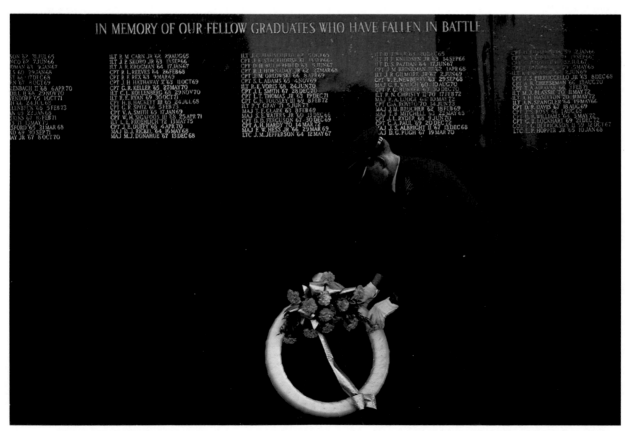

*Graduate War Memorial*

*Gimbel Collection , Academy Library*

*Class Reunion*

*Your experience at this magnificent institution, guided by honesty, integrity, and abiding loyalty to our nation will serve you well. These past four years have prepared you to take your place in the best darned Air Force in the world.*

President Ronald W. Reagan, Commencement, 1984

*Cadet Graduation*

*The mission of the Air Force Academy is to provide instruction and experience to all cadets so that they graduate with the knowledge and character essential to leadership and the motivation to become career officers in the United States Air Force.*

The United States Air Force Academy Mission

History of Flight

*Represented by the Gimbel Collection, 1493 Edition Book showing the first known illustration of the ICARUS; Balloon ascension over Milan, Italy, 1881 ; Aerial Meet ,Wien,  Germany, 1912; Lindbergh's New York to Paris trip, 1927 ; United States Air Force Academy Medal carried to the lunar surface by  the Apollo mission, 1971.*

# THE EARLY YEARS

*Photographs from the Air Force Academy archives*

*President Eisenhower signs the Academy Act. With him at the signing are Secretary of the Air Force Harold Talbott, Representative Fred Vinson, General Nathan Twining, Representative Dewey Short, Undersecretary James Douglas, Gen. Hubert Harmon*

*The Site Selection Commission in 1954. They are (left to right) Virgil Hancher, Gen. Hubert Harmon, Charles Lindbergh, Merill Meigs, Gen. Carl Spaatz and Gen. Curtis LeMay*

Gen. Hubert Harmon, the Academy's first Superintendent, signs General Order #1, activating the Academy, August 14, 1954

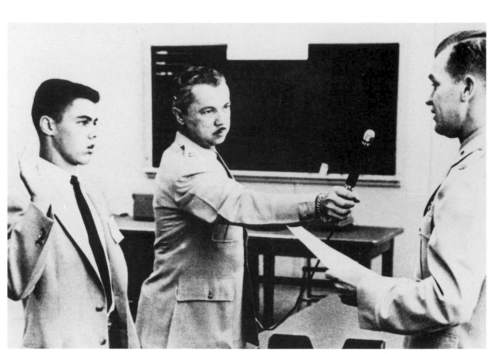

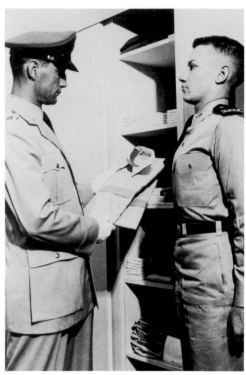

Valmore W. Bourque, the first cadet sworn into the Academy, July 11, 1955, was also the first Academy graduate to be killed in action

New cadet indoctrination

Lowry Air Force Base was the initial, temporary home of the Academy in the mid-1950s

*New cadets marching out of the headquarters building, Lowry AFB, 1955*

*It is said that the cadet training in the 50s...*

*...was as tough a regimen as there has ever been at the Academy*

*The dining hall at Lowry, ca. 1956*

*Chow time in the field*

*Cadets take live-fire training under the instruction of Air Force personnel, ca. 1956*

Cadet training did not neglect the traditional military arts, such as marching with full packs (right)

On June 3, 1959, 207 members of the first class of the Air Force Academy graduate, receiving their diplomas from Secretary of the Air Force James H. Douglas, and Commissions from Air Force Chief of Staff Gen. Thomas D. White (below)

*American aviators envisioned a "West Point of the air" from the time aircraft were introduced into America's military forces. That dream materialized in 1954 when the U.S.Air Force was only seven years old. In the years since the first class entered the United States Air Force Academy, many people have continued to combine their vision, talent and hard work to produce a thriving institution charged with producing the finest Air Force leaders in the world.*

Gen. Jerome F. O'Malley, June, 1984

*The Academy site near Colorado Springs prior to construction*

*The Academy site under construction in October, 1956. The first building under way at the site is Vandenberg Hall*

*The dining hall, academic buildings and cadet quarters under construction in 1957*

*The famous chapel under construction, 1961*

*Upper- class cadets arriving at the permanent site, August, 1958*

*President Lyndon Johnson signs the "Expansion Act" on March 3, 1964, increasing the size of the cadet wing . Looking on is Gen. C.V. Clifton*

## Falcons Do It Again! Cotton Bowl Is Next

### Will Face TCU In Dallas, Jan. 1

By DICK TUCKER
Free Press Sports Editor

BOULDER—The fabulous Falcons of the Air Force Academy capped an unbeaten football season Saturday afternoon with a come-from-behind 20-14 victory over Colorado University and a berth in the Cotton Bowl.

The Falcons accepted the bid to the Dallas New Year's Day classic immediately after the game. They'll play Southwest Conference champion Texas Christian in the post - season game.

Coach Ben Martin's crew turned CU mistakes into victory Saturday in a game that saw the Buffaloes from Boulder run up a huge statistical edge.

Seven CU fumbles turned the tide for the Falcons who stopped the Buffs for a final time just two yards short of the goal line with 11 seconds to play.

Third quarter touchdowns by halfbacks Mike Quinlan and Mike Rawlins reversed a 14-6 Colorado halftime lead. Then, the Academy twice stopped CU drives inside the 5 in the fourth quarter.

The victory gives the Falcons its first unbeaten, untied season in four years of existence. They recorded four unbeaten

**Sweetest Victory of the Year**

— Free Press-UPI Telephoto

...e, left, president of the Cotton Bowl Assn., shakes hands Saturday with All-America tackle Brock Strom, center, cap-... Air Force Academy football team, and Coach Ben Martin, right, after the Air Force accepted a bid to play Texas ... University in the Cotton Bowl Jan. 1. They're shown following the Air Force's 20-14 victory over Colorado University.

*The famous 1958 football team — Coach Ben Martin and tackle Brock Strom, the Academy's first football All-American*

*All-white dress uniforms at June Week, 1959*

*Julie Richards, among the first women to enter the Academy, as she arrives in 1976*

*Cadet Richards at graduation, 1980*

## HIGH FLIGHT

Oh, I have slipped the surly
  bonds of earth
And danced the skies
  on laughter-silvered wings;
Sunward I've climbed,
  and joined the tumbling mirth
Of sun-split clouds —
  and done a hundred things
You have not dreamed of —
  wheeled and soared and swung
High in the sunlit silence.
  Hov'ring there,
I've chased the shouting wind along
  and flung my eager craft
Through footless halls of air.
  Up, up the long,
Delirious burning blue
  I've topped the windswept heights
With easy grace
  where never lark,
Or even eagle flew.
  And, while with silent,
Lifting mind I've trod
  The high untrespassed
Sanctity of space,
  Put out my hand,
And touched the face of God.

— *John Gillespie Magee, Jr.*